BLACK COUNTRY
Wit & Humour

BRENDAN HAWTHORNE
AND
CAMILLA ZAJAC

BRADWELL
BOOKS

Published by Bradwell Books

9 Orgreave Close Sheffield S13 9NP

Email: books@bradwellbooks.co.uk

Complied by Brendan Hawthorne & Camilla Zajac

British Library Cataloguing in Publication Data: a catalogue record for
this book is available
from the British Library.

1st Edition

ISBN: 9781902674698

Print: Gomer Press, Llandysul, Ceredigion SA44 4JL

Design by: jenksdesign@yahoo.co.uk

Illustrations: ©Tim O'Brien 2013

Two council werkers on a site in Tipton am surveying land they'm about ter dig up. The gaffer says ter th'other 'un, " Yo goo an get the metal detector an check fer pipework. I'll get the kettle on an have a brew." The gaffer gets the tea gooin' while his maerte sets off werking.

Half-hour laerter the gaffer puts his paper down next to his mug of tea to find out how work is progressing and finds his mate sitting on a wall scrotchin his head. "Wots up wi yer?" The gaffer asks. "There's pipework all over the plaerce. Look!" The young worker sets off across the land, the bleeper sounding continuously as the detector passes in front of him. The gaffer loffs and says, "Am yo saft or what? Yo'm wearin steel toe caps in yer boots!"

Two old dears are suppin half pints of shandy in the passageway to the outdoor of a pub in Gornal. The one says to the other, "Was it love at fust sight when yo met yower owd mon?" "No I doe think so," came the reply, "I dae know ow much money he had when I fust met him!"

"Brothers and sisters have I none, yet that man's father is my father's son" who is "that man"?

That man is your son.

Harry proudly drove his new convertible into town and parked it on the main street, he was on his way to the Charity Shop to get rid of an unwanted gift, a foot spa, which he left on the back seat.

He had walked half way down the street when he realised that he had left the top down... with the foot spa in the back.

He ran all the way back to his car, but it was too late...
Another five foot spas had been dumped in the car.

Down the boozer a group of blokes sit around a table drinking when a mobile phone rings on the table. One of the men pick the phone up and puts the speaker phone on. A woman says "'Ow bin yer chap I hope you doe mind but I've just seen a diamond ring priced £2000 and wondered if I can buy it. I've got your credit card with me." "Of course my dear go ahead," anwswers the man. "While I'm on," purrs the lady, "I've noticed a top of the range car I'd like it's onny £65,000, could I order that an all?" "Of course my darling," replies the man. His friends around the table look at each other in disbelief as the lady continues, "And I've just noticed a house on the coast. It's onny £750,000 could we have that as well please?" "Of course my dear." Answers the man without so much as blinking. The phone call is ended and the man smiles as the others take a long swill of beer. Then suddenly the man looks up and shouts "Anyone know whose phone this is?"

A middle-aged couple from Walsall are sitting at the dining table in their semi-detached house talking about making preparations for writing their wills. Zac says to his missus, Edna, "I've bin thinking me wench if I goo fust ter meet me maker I don't want you ter be on yer own fer too long. In fact I think yo could do wuss than Col the sheet metal werker or Dave on the market. They'd look after yer when I ay here no more." "That's very kind on yer ter think about me like that Zac." Remarked Edna, " But I think yo should know that I've already made other arrangements!"

Six dozen dozen is greater than half a dozen dozen   yes or no?

No, both are equal.

After visiting the ballet Miss Malaprop was telling a colleague about the wonderful evening she had had the night before. On the production she commented how graceful the dancers were and how they had 'slid across the floor like they were on casternets!'

What is it that you can keep after giving it to someone else?

Your word

An Englishman, Irishman and a Scotsman walk into a bar.
The Barman says 'Is this a joke?'

One winter's night a lorry was drivin down the road in Oldbury when a car from Wednesbury behind it starts flashing its headlights and sounding its horn. This goes on for a good ten minutes before the car finally overtakes it on the dual carriageway and as it does so the driver from Wednesbury winds the window down and shouts to the lorry driver, "Oi mate yo'am losin yer load off the back."

"I bloomin well hope so!" The lorry driver shouts back. "I'm gritting the roads ay I!"

I give you a group of three. One is sitting down and will never get up. The second eats as much as is given to him, yet is always hungry. The third goes away and never returns. What are they?

A stove, fire and smoke.

Bloke sees his neighbour out gardening and goes to speak to him. 'Wot yo got there?" he asks him. "It's me grandfaerther's spaerde," answers the neighbour. I was justa thinken ow good a spaerde it's bin. It ay bin a minute's trouble." Interested, the bloke asks, "How old is it?" "A good eighty years old it is an in all that time it's onny had fower new handles and a new spade head!"

When one does not know what it is, then it is something; but when one knows what it is, then it is nothing?

A riddle.

Did you hear about the two men from the monastery who opened up a seafood restaurant? One was the fish friar, and the other was the chip monk.

Young lad gets home from a fishing trip down the Tame Valley cut. He carries his net in one hand and a jam jar in the other. His mutha asks, "How many fish yo catch son?" "Foive Mutha, look!" His mutha looks in the jar and counts four jack bannocks. "Yer fool, doe they teach yer ter count at at skewel? There's onny four fish in there" "Arr, the fifth un wuz a whale but I chucked it back cos it day av any spokes!"

What goes round the house and in the house but never touches the house?

The sun.

A vicar is conducting a wedding service and is droning on a bit when suddenly he asks the groom, "Will you take this woman to be your lawful wedded wife?" "That's what I'm here for ay ett?" replied the groom tersely.

When I am filled,
I can point the way;
When I am empty,
Nothing moves me.
I have two skins,
One without and one within.
What am I?

A glove.

Two boys were arguing when the teacher entered the room. The teacher says, 'Why are you arguing?'

One boy answers, 'We found a ten pound note and decided to give it to whoever tells the biggest lie.

'You should be ashamed of yourselves,' said the teacher, 'When I was your age I didn't even know what a lie was.'

The boys gave the ten pound note to the teacher.

Did you hear that they've crossed a Newfoundland and a Basset Hound? The new breed is a Newfound Asset Hound, a dog for financial advisors.

A bloke goes into an artist's studio and asks if the artist could paint a picture of him surrounded by beautiful and scantily clad women. The artist said that he could but was intrigued by such a strange request. When asked why he would want such a picture painted the bloke says, "Well if I die before me missus when she finds this painting she'll wonder which one I spent all me money on!"

A woman goes into an artist's studio and asks to be painted wearing a diamond necklace and earrings. "Of course madam. But why?" asked the artist. "Well if I die before me husband I want his new woman to be frantic searching for me jewellery!"

What comes once in a minute, twice in a moment, but never in a thousand years?

The letter M.

A pigeon fancier wakes up one morning to find his prize racer has got on wart on its head. Perturbed he goes to his neighbour to borrow a file. "What for?" asks the neighbour. "Me pigeon's got a wart on its yead. I need ter file it off." "You'll kill it filing its poor little yead." "I won't" replied the fancier, "I know what I'm adoin'" On returning the file the neighbour asks, "How's the pigeon?" "He died" replied the fancier, "Told yer e would." "Oh it wore the filin'," replied the fancier, "I think I tightened the vice too tight!"

What walks all day on its head?

A nail in a horse shoe.

A group of chess enthusiasts checked into a hotel and were standing in the lobby discussing their recent tournament victories. After about an hour, the manager came out of the office and asked them to move. 'But why?' they asked, as they walked off. 'Because,' he said 'I can't stand chess nuts boasting in an open foyer.'

Light as a feather?
Nothing in it.
Few can hold it.
For even a minute.

Your breath.

At the butcher's the trainee was serving a very posh lady with a freshly prepared chicken. As he handed her the chicken she noticed how dirty his arms were but how clean his hands were. "When you were taught to wash your hands, boy. Didn't they teach you to wash your arms as well?" " Oh I ain't washed me hands lady," answered the trainee, "I've been helpin the butcher clean the chickens out!"

The more you take, the more you leave behind. What are they?

Footsteps.

A drunk is swaying at the bar in an old spit and sawdust pub. He is rather the worse for drink. A new barman comes out from the back and sees that his first customer is already inebriated and is contemplating when to do when the drunk asks, " Giz a pint o treacle mild and a whisky chaser wust?" The young barman replies, "I'm really sorry, I can't serve you sir". The drunk re-focuses on his young friend and replies, "Well send me someone who can woolest!"

A man went on a trip on Friday, stayed for two days and returned on Friday. How is that possible?

Friday is a horse!

They say an Englishman laughs three times at a joke. The first time when everybody gets it, the second a week later when he thinks he gets it, the third time a month later when somebody explains it to him.

A man went into a hardware store and asked to buy a sink.
'Would you like one with a plug?' asked the assistant.
'Don't tell me they've gone electric,' said the man.

What always ends everything?

The letter 'g'.

In a factory in Bilston the blokes were treated to the sight of a young female office worker who liked to walk through the factory to the sound of wolf whistles. Everyday she walked through the factory when she could so easily have walked round the outside of the building. One day a Brummy went over to her and asked if she'd come to work on her bike that morning. Preening her hair she replied, "Why is my hair a mess this morning?" "No!" replied the Brummy. "It's just that I've noticed that you've got flies in your teeth!"

What five letter word can have its last four letters removed and still sound the same?

QUEUE - remove "UEUE", say Q. Q and queue are pronounced the same

This sad tale had a very serious sentiment but was somewhat lightened by the inherent malapropism. A lady was telling her friend how she had just got back from visiting her frail and elderly father in hospital. Her friend asked with reverence and care about the long term prognosis. "Oh, it's not good news, I'm afraid" said the lady about her father. "I mean, he's disintegrating rapidly!"

When is a yellow dog most likely to enter a house?

When the door is open.

In a street in Bilston the neighbours were out seeing what the new people were having done to their property. A big van turned up and all the stuff started to get taken in for what seemed to be a big diy project. Old Bill said to his son, "What's gooin on son?"

"It's the new bloke next dower dad, he's having a Jacuzzi I think." Old Bill replied, "I day know he could ride a motorbike!"

At a Christmas get together the in-laws had finished their meals, played their games, fallen asleep to the sound of the afternoon film, woken up ready for the next round of Christmas cheer to talk about which side if the family was better than the other. They went through best houses, best cars and best holidays. Then it started to get more personal. One family member says to his opposite "Well it's clear that our side has got the responsibility of having all the brains." "Pity they'm so addled!" was the knee jerk response.

What has a head like a cat, feet like a cat, a tail like a cat, but isn't a cat?

A kitten.

In the old days of steam trains a Black Country mon had finished his day at the office and ambled to the local railway station where he could just see the last of the carriages inching away from the platform. The ticket master challenged the passenger to see his ticket and as the passenger saw his train disappearing slowly down the track he finally found his ticket and was allowed on to the platform. "I con ketch it if I run hard enough." The passenger shouted and started to run after his train as it turned a bend and disappeared from view. The station master and ticket collector shook their heads and went into the tea room for a well earned rest. Half an hour later a bedraggled version of the man who was last seen chasing his train appeared in the tea room out of breath and weak at the knees. The ticket collector looked up and said, "Yo day manage ter catch it then did ya? I towd yo yo wouldn't." The passenger replied, 'Yo was…. err…..right mate…..errr….. but I dae half mek it puff!"

An old bloke at the bus stop outside Russells Hall Hospital is talkin to the next person in the queue whilst rubbing his head. "My wooden leg ay arf giving me some jip." The person in the queue looks at him and says, 'Really? Why?" The old man retorted, "Cos my missus keeps hitting me over the yead with it!"

I am so small, and sometimes I'm missed.
I get misplaced, misused, and help you when you list.
People usually pause when they see me.
So can you tell me what I could be?

A comma.

In the early days of television sets the ritual of switching the TV on and waiting for the valves to warm up was all part of building the excitement to watch a programme: usually the one that was on! Owd Jimmy Claypen from Ocker Hill decided to tell his naerbour about his newly acquired television and how he was going to watch the Queen's Coronation. "I've gorra goo in now ter watch the spectacle." He said looking at his pocket watch. His neighbour looked and said "But it ay on fer another three hours." "I know." said Jimmy, "but they'n sayin there'll be a lot there and I want ter get a good seat!"

What, when you need it you throw it away, but when you don't need it you take it back?

An anchor.

A duck walks into a pub and goes up to the barman.
The barman says 'What can I get you?'

Duck: 'Umm. Do you have any grapes?'
Barman (Looking surprised):

'No, I'm afraid we don't.'
The duck waddles slowly out of the pub.

The next day at the same time, the duck waddles into the pub, hops up on a bar stool.

Barman: 'Hi. What can I get for you?'
Duck: 'Um. Do you have any grapes?'

Barman (a little annoyed): 'Hey! Weren't you in here yesterday. Look mate, we don't have any grapes. OK?'

The duck hops off the stool and waddles out of the door.
The next day, at the same time, the barman is cleaning some glasses when

he hears a familiar voice
Duck: 'Umm.. Do you have any grapes?'

The barman is really annoyed
Barman: 'Look. What's your problem? You came in here yesterday asking for grapes, I told you, we don't have any grapes! Next time I see your little ducktail waddle in here I'm going to nail those little webbed feet of yours to the floor. GOT me pal?'

So the duck hops off the bar stool and waddles out.
The next day at the same time, the duck waddles into the pub, walks up to the barman and the barman says,
'
What on earth do YOU want?'
'Errrr. do you have any nails?'

'What!? Of course not.'
'Oh. Well, do you have any grapes?'

A bloke goes into a café on a Monday and asks for the all day breakfast. "But it's three o'clock in the afternoon!" complains the woman behind the counter getting ready to go home. After twenty minutes a plate is skimmed down in front of him. The bacon is burned, the sausage still pink. One egg is undercooked the other hard as a bibble. The fried bread is running with grease and the tomatoes are dry. His tea follows and is slopped on the table. The bloke eats what he can, pays and leaves. This happens everyday until Friday when the bloke congratulates the woman on her continued standard of excellence. The woman looks on and said in disbelief and says, "Everyday, after twenty minutes from you placing an order I skim the plate down in front of you. The bacon is burned, the sausage still pink. One egg is undercooked, the other hard as a bibble. The fried bread is running with grease and the tomatoes are dry. Your tea follows which I slop on the table, I have been rude to you and showed no compassion towards you at all." The bloke looks at her and says, "Well at least yo'am consistent which is mower than can be said about a lot round eya!"

A Sedgely golfer was going around the course talking to his caddy for the day between holes about an up and coming competition. "I've been drawn against Jack Smith form Gornal, is he any good?" The caddy checked for a moment and said, " He's absolutely rubbish. Can't get around the course with any ease. He set a new course record for the worst round ever that has only just been beaten." "Oh, I should easily get through to the next round then, shan't I?" The caddy looked down at the score card and said, "I wouldn't bet on it!"

What jumps when it walks and sits when it stands?

A kangaroo.

A man wanted to become a monk so he went to the monastery and talked to the head monk.

The head monk said, 'You must take a vow of silence and can only say two words every three years.'

The man agreed and after the first three years, the head monk came to him and said, 'What are your two words?'

'Food cold!' the man replied.
Three more years went by and the head monk came to him and said 'What are your two words?'

'Robe dirty!' the man exclaimed.
Three more years went by and the head monk came to him and said, 'What are your two words?'

'I quit!' said the man.
'Well', the head monk replied, 'I'm not surprised. You've done nothing but complain ever since you got here!'

Ethel and Sid are having matrimonial difficulties and seek the advice of a counsellor. The couple are shown into a room where the counsellor asks Ethel, in her mind, what problems she faces in her relationship with Sid. "Well," she starts, "he shows me no affection, I don't seem to be important to him anymore. We don't share the same interests and I don't think he loves me anymore." Ethel has tears in her eyes as the counsellor walks over to her, gives her a big hug and kisses her firmly on the lips. Sid looks on in passive disbelief. The counsellor turns to Sid and says, "This is what Ethel needs once a day for the next month. Can you see that she gets it?" Sid looks unsettled, " Well I con drap her off everyday other than Wednesdays when I play snooker and Sundays when I goo fishing!"

What has five eyes, but cannot see?

The Mississippi River.

Three Black Country bears from a ground floor flat in Tipton go for a walk around the local park. On their return mother bear says to father bear, "Did yo leave the kitchen winder open faerther bear?" "I dae, mutha bear it wort me." So mother bear turns to babby bear and says, "Babby bear did yo leave the kitchen winder open?" "I dae, mutha bear, it wort me." So the three bears go into their flat worrying about what they might find. Three bowls are on the table set with cutlery. Faerther bear says, " Well whoever it is ay touched me bowl of faggits and pays: they'm still here." As he sits down to eat, mutha bear says, "My bowl of faggits and pays um still here an all. They ay bin touched neither." And she sits down to eat. Babby bear looks round and says, "Stuff the faggits and pays. Somebody's nicked the widescreen TV!"

One Sunday morning two blokes, Dominic and Sebastian, from Great Barr, are on their adjoining drives talking about their new cars. Dominic says to Sebastian, "I see you've had one of those new electric cars. Is it economical to run?" "Oh yes," replied Sebastian, "It only cost me 25 pence to drive to Manchester and back the other day." "Wow, that's really good." replied Dominic. "Only drawback is," continued Sebastian, "the electric cable to get from here to there cost twenty-five thousand pounds!"

What was given to you, belongs to you exclusively and yet is used more by your friends than by yourself?

Your name.

A passenger in a taxi tapped the driver on the shoulder to ask him something.

The driver screamed, lost control of the cab, nearly hit a bus, drove up over the curb and stopped just inches from a large plate glass window. For a few moments everything was silent in the cab, then the driver said, 'Please, don't ever do that again. You scared the daylights out of me.'

The passenger, who was also frightened, apologised and said he didn't realize that a tap on the shoulder could frighten him so much, to which the driver replied, 'I'm sorry, it's really not your fault at all. Today is my first day driving a cab. I've been driving a hearse for the last 25 years.'

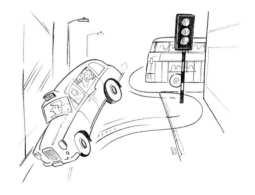

Three Black Country blokes am getting drunk in a pub in Cradley. One of them says, "When I'm jed and the family come round ter see me lyin in state at the wake I hope they say, "He wort a bad 'un. Had his faults but the money was on the kitchen taerble every pay day." The second bloke sups his beer thoughtfully and says, "When ma lot come round me I want 'em ter say that I was honest and although I didn't have a full day's werk in me I still looked after everybody as well as I could." The two blokes turn to the third who puts his glass down and says, " Well I hope my lot say, "Look eya! He's still abreathin' by the look on it!"

What time does Sean Connery arrive at Wimbledon?
Tennish.

What do you get if you cross a nun and a chicken?
A pecking order!

Why is a clock like a depressed person?
It's forever running itself down!

Three Black Country women talking in a bar about a party they've been invited to. The fustun says, "We've gotta wear summat that matches our husbands ay we at this party?" "Are," said the other two. The fustun continued, "Well my husband's got black hair and I've got a little black dress I can diet into be then." The secondun says, "That's a good idea. My husband has got brown hair and I've got a brown dress I can diet into by then an all." The thirdun looks a bit hesitant and says " I just need to go on a diet: My husbands bald!"

The leader of a leading vegetarian society just couldn't control himself any more. He just needed to try some pork, just to see what it tasted like. So one summer day he told his members he was going away for a break. He left town and headed to the nearest restaurant. After sitting down, he ordered a roasted pig, and impatiently waited for his delicacy. After just a few minutes, he heard someone call his name, and to his horror he saw one of his fellow members walking towards him. Just at that same moment, the waiter walked over, with a huge platter, holding a full roasted pig with an apple in its mouth. 'Isn't that something,' says the man after only a moment's pause, 'All I do is order an apple, and look what it comes with!'

A man is rushing to a hospital from a business trip because his wife has just gone into labour with twins, and there is a family tradition that the first family member to arrive gets to name the children. The man is afraid his wayward brother will show up first and give his kids horrible names. When he finally arrives at the hospital in a cold sweat he sees his brother sitting in the waiting room, waving, with a silly grin on his face. He walks unhappily in to see his wife who is scowling and holding two little babies, a boy and a girl. Almost afraid to hear it, the man asks, 'What did he name the girl?' 'Denise' says the wife. 'Hey that's not too bad! What did he name the boy?' 'De-nephew.'

Two blokes standing in the dole queue waiting for their turn at the counter. First bloke says to the second one, "I have to buy my wife something for our wedding anniversary and the dole cheque won't cover it." The second bloke looks up from his paper and says, "What date?" The first bloke thinks for a while and says, "15th September." The second bloke considers his next question. "What year?" Without taking a breath the first bloke retorts, "Every year for the last twenty seven!"

What lies at the bottom of the ocean and twitches?

A nervous wreck.

What's the difference between roast beef and pea soup?

Anyone can roast beef.

A man walks into a doctor's office with two onions under his arms, a potato in his ear and a carrot up his nose. He asks the doctor: 'What's wrong with me?'

The doctor replies: 'You're not eating properly.'

A mon from Princes End goos down the phone box and makes a call for a mid-wife to attend as his missus is going through the final stages of labour. He runs back wum to comfort his missus when suddenly a new mid-wife, out on her inaugural call, bursts in through the bedroom door all flushed and ready to deliver. The woman screams out as the baby makes a move. The young mid-wife, trying to think of something to say, says, "Is this your first one?" "No you fool!" screamed the woman, "This is me husband!"

All about, but cannot be seen,
Can be captured, cannot be held,
No throat, but can be heard.
What is it?

The wind.

A girl who was just learning to drive went down a one-way street
in the wrong direction, but didn't break the law. How come?

She was walking.

I'm part of the bird that's not in the sky. I can swim in the ocean and yet remain dry. What am I?

A shadow.

A man builds a house rectangular in shape. All the sides have southern exposure. A big bear walks by. What colour is the bear? Why?

The bear is white because the house is built on the North Pole.

A new client had just come in to see a famous lawyer.

'Can you tell me how much you charge?', said the client.

'Of course', the lawyer replied, 'I charge £200 to answer three questions!'

'Well that's a bit steep, isn't it?'

'Yes it is,' said the lawyer, 'And what's your third question?'

What kind of ears does an engine have?

Engineers

Two neighbourly women, Madge and Dot, fell out one day whilst arguing about overgrowing trees. They didn't spake fer months until one day Madge, who was the more forgiving of the two ladies, heard Dot in the garden and called over, "Is that yo Dot?" "No it ay!" Dot shouted back. "Well it ay me then neither!" shouted back Madge. And so the sulk continued between both neighbours!

What kind of coat can only be put on when wet?

A coat of paint.

How many surrealists does it take to screw in a lightbulb?
Banana.

What does one star say to another star when they meet?
Glad to meteor!

What can you catch but not throw?

.bloↃ A

Two aerials meet on a roof - fall in love - get married. The ceremony was rubbish - but the reception was brilliant.

What do you do if you are driving your car in central London and you see a space man?

Park in it, of course.

Two blokes walking along the tow path of the cut. One's a big un and the other a thin weedy un. The big un says, "Bet yo ten bob I con chuck yo from this side o the cut to the tother." "I bet yo cor," says the thin un. "I'd like ter see yo try." "Come here!" says the big un grabbing one arm and leg of the thin un. The big un proceeds to spin the thin un around and finally lets him go. There's a big splash and eventually the thin un rises ter the surface of the dark cut waerter and splutters, " See yo couldn't do it. Yo owe me ten bob!" The big un shouts back, "I doe. I day say I could do it fust time!"

You can have me but cannot hold me.
Gain me and quickly lose me.
If treated with care I can be great.
And if betrayed I will break.
What am I?

Trust.

Why couldn't Cinderella be a good soccer player?

She lost her shoe, she ran away from the ball, and her coach was a pumpkin.

What do you call a boomerang that won't come back?

A stick.

What gets wetter and wetter the more it dries?

A towel.

What goes around the world but stays in a corner?

A stamp.

I have holes in my top and bottom, my left and right and in the middle. What am I?

A sponge.

My life can be measured in hours;
I serve by being devoured.
Thin, I am quick; fat, I am slow.
Wind is my foe.
What am I?

A candle.

Labourer shouts up to his roofer mate on top of an owd terraced house and says, "Doe yo get climbing down this ladder, Burt." "Why not?" shouts back Burt. "Cos I moved it five minutes agoo!' replied his mate.

Two blokes walking home from different steel tube werks. The first bloke says, 'We mek tubes that big as the hole darn em weighs five tons." The second bloke replies, "Ours em that lickle yo cor see the hole at all cos we atta werk ter thousandths of an inch." The first bloke looks puzzled and asks, "How many thousandths of an inch em in an inch then?" The second bloke thinks for a minute and says, "I don't really know. I ay actually counted 'em but there must be millions!"

The family arrive at the church for the christening of their latest family member. The vicar stands at the font and before he precedes in naming the infant asks aloud, "Was this child born in wedlock?" "Nah!" came a shout from the back of the group. "He was born in Gospel Oak".

An old Tipton sportin mon goos down to the bookies to put a bet on. He decides ter take his Jack Russell terrier with him for a walk. As the dog was under age ter goo in the bookies our mon ties his dog to a lamp post outside the shop. As he leaves the bookies he see that only the dog's lead remains tied to the lamp post. His mate stops to ask him if he's ok as he looks a bit ashen. "I've onny bin in there five minutes. Me dog was tied ter that lamp post an when I come out there he wuz, gone!"

A man enters a dark cabin. He has just one match with him. There is an oil lamp, a wood stove, and a fireplace in the cabin. What would he light first?

The match.

What is it that never asks you any questions and yet you answer?

Your phone.

Your mother's brother's only brother-in-law is your Stepfather, Grandfather, Uncle or Father?

Your Father.

What gear were you in at the moment of the impact?

Gucci sweats and Reeboks.

What's green and runs around the garden?

A hedge.

How do you make a sausage roll?

Push it!

Many years ago on the owd LMS railway line in Wednesbury a young recruit was given the job of filling the signal lamps on the station. He got all the clear lamps and promptly readied them for the night's work by trimming wicks and polishing the lenses. When the stationmaster came in to the lamp room to see how the young man was doing he noticed him rifling through cupboards and cabinets vainly looking for something. "What yo lookin fer son?" the station master enquired. "Well,' said the young man, "I'm lookin fer the red oil.""The red oil?" questioned the station master. "We ay got any red oil. What yo want it fer anyway?" The young man stopped searching and replied, "Well I've filled the clear lamps with clear oil. Now I'm looking fer red oil fer the red lamps!"

Why do seagulls live by the sea?

Because if they lived by the bay they would be called bagels.

Why was the scarecrow promoted?

He was outstanding in his field!

What is the longest word in the English language?

Smiles. Because there is a mile between its first and last letters.

A thin and rather straggly man from a local government office is trying to encourage people to plant food crops in their gardens to save on food miles. He takes it upon himself to go on a tour of local organisations in the borough to spread his vision to the masses. Dressing to impress he dons a rather ill-fitting suit and sets off to talk to the first group of the general public at their local library in Wednesbury. His talk goes down well and is confident for the question and answer session that he's set up to follow his presentation. Owd Joe puts his hand up in order to ask a question. The man from the council says, "And our first question is from the gentleman on the front row. Yes sir, what is your question?" "Well," says owd Joe. "Yo'ave spun we a good tale o wot we'm sposed ter do but how con you help we practically ter put all this yo'n talked about into action?" The man from the council looked shocked at the direct question and answered, "I'm an ideas man and not very practical so I don't see what help I could offer in that sense." Molly from the audience chimed in, " Don't put yerself down me mon, yo'd mek a bostin scarcrow."

A Black Country mon goes to Hawaii for his holidays and is sitting on the beach in his floral shirt and shorts drinking a cooling drink under the shade of an umbrella. Just on it a bloke walks past with a plank of wood under his arm. "What's that plank o wood yo got under yer arm aer maerte?" asks our intrepid Black Country mon. The bloke replies, "It's a surfboard.""Oh is it?" replies the Black Country mon still confused. Anyway he carries on drinking and watches the bloke go to the water's edge and swim out with his plank of wood. Just on it the bloke stands up on the board and rides a big curling wave before getting knocked off it by a big roll of sea. The bloke walks back up the beach and past our Black Country mon who asks, "What did yo say that plank was called again?""A surfboard," replies the bloke. The Black Country mon scratches his head and comments, "Well when yo fell off just it dae look very saerfe ter me!"

Why was the computer so tired when it got home?
Because it had a hard drive!

What do you get when you cross a dog with a telephone?
A Golden Receiver!

A bloke has just finished painting the windowsills of his terraced house in Ocker Hill when he discovers he has nothing to clean his brushes with. Off he goes to the local convenience store and asks if the shopkeeper has got any turps. "What sort of taerps done thee want?" asked the shop keeper. "Video or audio?"

When's a seed like a fencepost?

When it prop a gates!

What do cats like to eat for breakfast?

Mice Krispies

An interior designer walks into the barber's shop and asks, "Where did you get that stripy paint from on your pole?"

Joby Smith is an industrial builder and is repairing the masonry around the top rim of a smokestack belonging to a local forge. He stands up on the brick rim and shouts down to his mate Sid that he wants him to join him. Sid doesn't have a head for heights and ignores Joby's call. Every few minutes Sid hears a call from the top of the stack and begins to wonder if his mate is ok. Reluctantly and cautiously he begins his climb on the small fitted access ladders ever upwards towards his mate. As he reaches the top Joby says, "Come here quick, Sid!" "What is it Joby?" Pants Sid, shaking and clinging to the ladder." Bin yer awright me mon? It's alright I'm here now.""Are I'm fine Sid thanks. I just wanted ter tell ya ow quiet it is up here on yer own and show ya ow far I could see!"

Ten women on a hen night decide that one of them should stay more sober than the other nine and look after the money to pay for their drinks. After deciding who would hold the money they all put twenty pounds into the kitty to cover expenses. After many drinks they stood around after closing time to divvy up the leftover cash. "How do we stand?" said Lottie from Dudley. "That's the easy part!" said Connie from Halesowen. "I'm wondering how I can walk. I've missed the last bus home!"

A bloke walks up to the foreman of a road laying gang and asks for a job. " I ay got one fer yer terday." Says the foreman looking up from his newspaerper. "But if yo walk half a mile down here yo con see if yo like the werk an I con put yer on the list fer tomorrer. "That's great mate," said the bloke as he wandered off down the road to find the gang. At the end of the shift the bloke walked past the foreman and shouted, "Ta maert, see ya tomorrer." The foreman looked up from his paper and shouted back, "Yo've enjoyed theeself then?" "Are I have!" shouted back the bloke, " But con I have a shovel or a pick ter lean on like the rest o the gang?"

A new recruit starts as a trainee manager in a supermarket and after a three month trial period the store manager is asked by the regional manager how the new recruit is doing and whether they've settled in to their new role and have all the necessary know how to broaden their career. The store manager replies, scratches his head for a moment and replies " Know how. Know how I've gone through it all and told im all I know and now he doe know anything so I think he'll be fine to work here!"

I am seen in places that appear to need me not.
I come seldom to places that need me most.
Sometimes my arrival is celebrated,
at others times I am hated.
I refresh all things whether they need it or not.

Rain.

Two Black Country blokes, Bob and Jim, goo on a skiing trip to Switzerland. Their first day is spent on the starter slopes and they are on their way towards the aprez ski when a pile of snow drops off the roof of the lodge. Bob looks at the drift of snow that has engulfed his mate and starts digging away at the icy blob with his hands shouting, "Jim! Jim! Con yo hear me? Am yer awright? Bin yo jed Bob? "I bay jed Jim," Bob called back, "but I'm that shocked I cor spake!"

A man walks into a bookshop and says 'I hope you don't have a book on reverse psychology.'

Two snowmen are standing in a field. One says to the other 'That's funny, I can really smell carrots.'

If vegetarians eat vegetables, what do humanitarians eat?

Language student to teacher, 'Are 'trousers' singular or plural?'
Teacher, 'They're singular on top and plural on the bottom.'

Jack from Darlaston got on the bus with his hands held out in front of him about a foot apart. The conductor comes up to him and says, "Giz yer fare Jack?" "I cort" came the reply. "I'll pay yer on the way back." The conductor looked puzzled and said, "I'll get the sack if the inspector gets on. I gorra have yer fare now!" "That's nothing to what I'll get when I goo um" reasoned Jack "an atta tell the missus ter measure the winder I bost this morning again!"

A rent collector goes to a small holding on a farm and knocks the door of the humble tied cottage. A young boy opens the door and asks what business the man has on his parents property. " I've come to collect the rent me lad. Where's thee faerther?" " Yo cort spake to him, he's busy." "I shall speak to him. He owes me rent." Came the reply. "Well he's feeding the pigs at the moment. Yo'll be able to tell me faerther easy enough though. He's the one wearing a hat!"